HOW TO CREATE A PERFORMANCE WORK STATEMENT

GUIDANCE FOR WRITING PROPER STATEMENTS OF WORK FOR PERFORMANCE

By: Robert Kurt Knauer

Copyright © 2016

Cover by Robert Knauer

ISBN-13: 978-1539812678   ISBN-10: 1539812677

All rights reserved. This book may not be reproduced, or shared without the express written consent of the author and owner of the copyright. For agencies, or commercial firms wishing to have the author come teach a one-time class, reproduction is authorized for such one-time events.

DISCLAIMER: This work is a generic work about how contracts are administered by the federal government in relation to vendor contracts and can be applied to state and local government contracting situations too. Work is that of the author, who is a former professor of contracts for the Defense Acquisition University, Defense Civilian Personnel Support Office, and Navy Acquisition Management Training Office. The Author used public records, the Federal Acquisition Regulations and his own professional knowledge to put this work together. This book and its eBook are licensed for your personal enjoyment and knowledge. Both the book and eBook may not be resold or copied to be given away to others. If you would like to share this book with anyone else, please purchase an additional copy for each recipient, or obtain specific written permission from the author. Thank you for respecting the hard work of the author. You may purchase this book through numerous resellers of 'Create Space', Amazon and

Kindle eBooks. Soon it will be released in audio book format via Amazon "Audible."

About the Author: Mr. Robert Kurt Knauer served as naval supply corps officer, senior contracting officer and trainer for the Department of Defense, Department of Labor, U.S. Department of Transportation, and numerous commercial firms. His contracting experience spans not only 32 years in the federal government, but an additional 7 years as Chief Executive Officer of "The Acquisition Institute, Incorporated" a consulting and training firm in which he increased sales by over 200% each year for seven straight years before retiring. He taught PWS Development courses to over 4000 federal employees, and wrote numerous articles and papers on the subject.

Dedication: It took several years after I retired as CEO to finish this guidebook. My inspiration in doing so is based upon my last government supervisor, Mr. Thomas Kaplan, also now retired, who always told me I should write what I know about best. I also give thanks to my wife for leaving me alone to finish it.

Preface

The objective of this guide is to provide guidance and assistance to our technical and program customers when it is necessary to develop a statement of work for any procurement. This document provides guidance, instructions and references for the preparation of performance work statements for government and commercial acquisitions. Although it provides coverage for statements of work in general, it emphasizes the use of Performance (Based) Work Statements or rather Performance Work Statements (PWS). It is general policy that all contracts will be considered for a PWS and focus on outcomes or results and not methods of performance or processes per se. Acquisition reform has been ongoing since 1983 in government. It strives to reduce risk by using performance-based specifications and standards, which make any contractor and sub-contractor responsible for providing the product as requested, assuming the risk for meeting performance requirements, and seeking innovations to efficiently and effectively achieve performance objectives. Contractors are given wide latitude for determining the best methods of performance, with more responsibility for performance quality. The use of PWS should lead to more cost-effective acquisitions and better value no matter who uses them (vendor or a government body).

BASIC BOOK INFORMATION	1
PREFACE	3
TABLE OF CONTENTS	4
CHAPTER 1: REQUIREMENT DOCUMENTS	6
GENERAL	6
ALTERNATIVES TO A STATEMENT OF WORK	7
STATEMENTS OF WORK	7
KINDS OF STATEMENTS	8
POLICY	10
CHAPTER 2: PERFORMANCE WORK STATEMENT CONSIDERATIONS	11
ADVANCE PLANNING	11
Market Research	11
Early Communication with Industry	12
PREPARATION GUIDANCE	13
General	13
Deliverables	17
Data Requirements	18
Use of Property	19
PROTECTING THE INTEGRITY OF THE PROCESS	20
KEY PARTICIPANTS	21
Project Manager	21
Contracting Officer (CO) or authorized commercial official	21
Contracting Officer's Representative	22
Quality Assurance Representative (QAR)	22
CHAPTER 3: REQUIREMENTS ANALYSIS	23
GETTING STARTED	23
WORK BREAKDOWN STRUCTURES (WBS)	23
GATHERING HISTORICAL DATA	24
Benchmarking	25
Output Data	26
Physical Resources Data	26
Personnel Resources Data	26
Quality Systems Data	26
PROJECT WORK BREAKDOWN STRUCTURES (PWBS)	27

CONTRACT WORK BREAKDOWN STRUCTURES (CWBS)	28
Extension of the CWBS by Contractors	30
Contractual Use of the CWBS	31
PURCHASER COST ESTIMATES	32
CHAPTER 4: PERFORMANCE WORK STATEMENTS (PWS)	34
GENERAL	34
Routine Services	36
Non-Routine Requirements	37
GUIDELINES FOR WRITING A PWS	38
Hardware or End Item Deliverables	39
Performance Based Specification	39
Systems Contracts	42
Support Services	43
Research and Development (R&D) Contracts	45
Basic Research	46
APPENDICES	
APPENDIX A: Document Review Checklist	47
APPENDIX B: Definitions	49
APPENDIX C: Acronym List	53
APPENDIX D: PBC Performance Standards and Incentives	54

CHAPTER 1

REQUIREMENTS DOCUMENTS

GENERAL

In order to acquire goods, services, research, products and other items through the PWS process, needs must be described to contractors, suppliers and vendors properly. This description is called a specification, needs statement or statement of work or performance work statement. In the Federal government, Federal Acquisition Regulation (FAR) (Part 11) prescribes policies and procedures for describing agency needs. It has established an order of priority that requirement documents, such as statements of work, should be "performance-oriented". The next type of needs document is a "detailed design-oriented" document. Lastly, the FAR lists government standards and specifications as the least preferred type of needs document.

Developing a needs or requirements document can be a very complex and challenging task. Statements of work are the most challenging of the requirements documents. Normally a statement of work is employed when the simpler needs requirements documents cannot be used and it must describe in sufficient detail what must be accomplished. The statement of work must be done properly and with high quality. Contracting for timely, high quality products or services is wholly dependent on the statement of work or requirements document. If the needs are not <u>well described</u> it is highly likely that a contractor (supplier) will have difficulty producing what your purchasing agency needs to support YOUR mission.

As a result, this guidance is being issued to assist technical and program personnel in writing the most difficult requirements document, the statement of work.

ALTERNATIVES TO A STATEMENT OF WORK – THE PWS

Once a requirement of need has been identified, it is possible that a requirements document or statement of work may not be necessary. There are a number of initiatives that may save time and effort by using existing contracts or a streamlined acquisition method.

For small dollar procurements credit cards can now be used. Should a requirement fit into the credit card program, a very short and succinct statement may be all that is needed.

Acquiring commercial items and services is another method of procurement that eliminated the need for a formal statement of work which usually doesn't work well. The principle employed here is that purchasing agencies acquire supplies and services from the commercial sector the way they sell to each other. A statement of need is developed which explains to industry what needs to be accomplished, the type of product or service to be acquired, the performance requirements and/or the essential physical characteristics. It is also the preferred manner in which to conduct an acquisition. Should your requirement appear to meet this commercial items method it offers shorter procurement lead time and other advantages.

STATEMENTS OF WORK

Statements of work are the most essential documents in any Federal solicitation or contract. They are read and interpreted by government and industry personnel with diverse backgrounds such as engineers, scientists, accountants, lawyers, contract specialists and other business fields. Therefore, the statements of work must be written so that technical and non-technical readers can understand them during the solicitation, award and administration phases of the acquisition cycle. An initial investment of time and effort to write a clear and high quality statement of work will:

a. enable offerors to clearly understand the requirements and needs of an agency or firm;

b. allow offerors to more accurately cost or price their proposal and submit higher quality technical proposals;

c. provide a baseline for the development of other parts of the solicitation, particularly the evaluation criteria, technical proposal instructions and independent cost estimate;

d. minimize the need for change orders which can increase the cost or price and delay completion;

e. allow both the government and contractors to assess performance; and

f. reduce claims and disputes under the contract.

KINDS OF STATEMENTS OF WORK (SOW)

There are three types of specifications, they are:

a. **Design/detailed** specifications;

b. **Level of effort** specifications; and

c. **Performance Work Statements**, known as a PWS

Although there are other types and variations of each, this guide will work within these three categories.

Design/detail statements of work tell the contractor how to do the work. It may include precise measurements, tolerances, materials, quality control requirements, and other government requirements that control the processes of the contractor. There are wide variances in application of this type of SOW. It is as varied as the requirements that are acquired under them. The point is that the government, to a large degree, requires the contractor to follow the government's way of performing the task or making a product. This causes the risk of performance to be borne by the government. For instance, if the contractor builds and/or performs a task and follows the government's SOW exactly, and the product or service is faulty, who is to blame? Absent malfeasance or shoddy workmanship it is the government's process that the contractor was implementing so the contractor cannot be faulted. Although this type of SOW is primarily used for manufacturing or construction, other work efforts are described in this rigid format.

Level-of-effort Statements of Work can be written for almost any type of service unless it is an inherent government function. The real deliverable under this type of contract is an hour of work. They are normally associated with task order and delivery order contracts. Services or products are acquired via individual orders issued by the Contracting Office. The SOWs are usually very broad and describe the general nature, scope or complexity of the services or products to be procured over a given period of time. It is important in writing these SOWs to assure all work items are sufficiently covered. Task orders or delivery orders can only be issued in those areas specifically covered in the SOW. All activities outside of the SOW must be acquired through a separate procurement action.

Performance-based statements of work or Performance Work Statements are the preferred method of stating needs. A performance based statement of work structures all aspects of an acquisition around the purpose of the work to be performed and does not dictate how the work is to be accomplished. It is written to ensure that contractors are given the freedom to determine how to meet the Government's performance objectives and provides for payment only when the results meet or exceed these objectives. It maximizes contractor control of work processes and allows for innovation in approaching various work requirements. Performance based SOWs <u>emphasize performance</u> that can be contractually defined so that the results of the contractor's effort can be measured in terms of technical and quality achievement, schedule progress, or cost performance. The goal of a PWS is to:

a. Save money by reducing contract costs from elimination of unnecessary effort, through innovation by the contractor or vendor, and also by reducing amount of overall surveillance needed.

b. It enables buyers and sellers to shift its emphasis from processes to outputs.

c. Hold vendors accountable for the end results. Ensure that contractors are given the freedom to determine how to meet performance objectives.

POLICY

It has been policy since 1983 for all new government contracts for services, hardware, and research and development will be considered for suitability for Performance Based Contracting and focus on required outcomes or results, not methods of performance or processes. Justification is required for the use of other than PBC or PWS methods when acquiring services.

CHAPTER 2

PERFORMANCE WORK STATEMENT CONSIDERATIONS

ADVANCE PLANNING

Attention to the early stages of program and procurement planning is critical to achieving a successful acquisition. Identify and contact your Contracting representative or chief of procurement. Inform them of what you are planning and ask for any suggestions. Keep them informed as you progress. There may be items such as, reporting requirements, market research, appropriateness of contract type, and the incorporation of effective incentive provisions that relate to your requirement that the contracting office can help you with. The amount of planning will be proportional to the complexity of the contemplated procurement. Program and Project Offices must determine what work will be performed by contractors. The SOW or PWS should be structured so that it is conducive to efficient performance. Vendors must be given complete and severable pieces of work for which they will be held accountable by contract. It is much easier to write a PWS around an output if a complete task is turned over to the contractor and they are held responsible.

Market Research

In the federal government, agencies are required by Part 10 of the Federal Acquisition Regulation (FAR) to ensure that legitimate needs are identified and trade-offs evaluated to acquire items that meet those needs. Market research is much easier for commercial vendors to perform. It can include the Project Officer's knowledge of the marketplace, information gleaned from prior acquisitions, or come from a formal sources sought notices published. FAR Parts 11 and 12 require government buyers to buy a commercial product or service if feasible. If a commercial item is not available, the requirement must be reviewed to see if it can be revised to encompass commercial items.

Early Communication with Industry Vendors

Work with the contracting office to determine whether to release draft SOW or PWS and other solicitation documents. This pre-release is recommended and has the following advantages:

> (1) permits early industry review and comment on complex specifications or PWS,
>
> (2) promotes competition,
>
> (3) encourages informal resolution of procurement problems,
>
> (4) improves industry's understanding of requirements and evaluation criteria, and
>
> (5) encourages proposers to replace government standards with non-Government standards.

Normally a draft solicitation is issued to permit early identification and resolution of industry's questions, concerns, and recommendations. Conferences calls with prospective offerors can also be held to clarify or explain requirements or to address industry questions or recommendations on how to state those requirements. These may be Pre-solicitation Conferences (held before release of the solicitation) or Pre-proposal Conferences (held after release of the solicitation but before proposals are due).

PREPARATION GUIDANCE

This section provides suggestions for developing and writing statements of work. The suggestions are organized by topic.

General

a. The PWS will be read and interpreted by a variety of people from diverse disciplines, such as attorneys, acquisition personnel, cost estimators, accountants, technical specialists, engineers, etc. It is imperative that the words be understood not only by the writer of the PWS, but by the readers.

b. The PWS or specification, as an integral part of a contract, is subject to contract law. A fundamental legal principle is that because the government is the drafter, any ambiguity usually is construed against the Government by the courts; that is, when two reasonable interpretations are possible, the court will adopt the interpretation espoused by the non-drafting party. The interpreter must look to what the contract actually says, not what the Government meant to say or would like to have said. When commercial contractors draft language it is not as simple, courts must look to industry terminology and industry standards. Often drafters of PWS are often tempted to write vague language because they think it gives them the flexibility to loosely interpret the PWS at a later date. However, the drafter would lose in a contract dispute based on an ambiguity in the PWS. Further, ambiguous work statements result in protests, unsatisfactory contractor performance, delays, claims, disputes, and increased contract costs.

Conversely, a high-quality document leads to a greater likelihood of successful contractor performance. When drafting any PWS, strive for clarity.

c. Simple words, phrases, and sentences are used for clarity. Well-understood words and phrases improve the PWS by minimizing ambiguities. Be concise, precise, and consistent. Careful and exact descriptions will avoid misunderstandings before and during the life of a contract. Keep sentences short and to the point.

d. Choice of Verbs.

> (1) **Use Active verbs**. Examples include: analyze, audit, calculate, create, design, develop, erect, evaluate, explore, interpret, investigate, observe, organize, perform, and produce (work words). For instance, the PWS could require the contractor to "conduct the experiment and produce a report describing and analyzing (or interpreting) the results."
>
> (2) **Avoid Passive verbs** that can lead to vague statements. For example, the phrase "the contractor shall perform," is preferred in lieu of "it shall be performed" because the latter does not definitively state which party shall perform. Avoid "should" or "may" because they leave the decision for action up to the contractor. Use "shall" when describing a provision binding on the contractor. Use "will" to indicate actions by the Government.

e. To reduce the possibility of misinterpretation, terminology must be consistent. The same words and phrases must be used when describing the same requirement. It is confusing if a hole is referred to as an "orifice" and later called an "aperture".

f. When contracting for services, they chief procurer must ensure that any final action reflects the informed, independent judgment of higher officials. Decision making includes activities that require either the exercise of discretion in applying authority or the making of value judgments in forming decisions.

g. Avoid redundancy. Redundancy can reduce clarity, thereby increasing the possibility for ambiguity and contradiction. If amplification, modification, or exceptions are required, make specific reference to the applicable portions and describe the change.

h. Vague/inexact words and generalizations are open to so many interpretations that they become meaningless. Phrases such as "securely mounted", "properly assembled", and "carefully performed" are examples of unenforceable language. Avoid catch-all and open-ended phrases, such as "is common practice in the industry," "as directed," or "subject to approval."

i. Note that common industry or in-house terminology is not always as universally defined as might be assumed. Technical terms must be specifically defined since judges settling disputes lean toward the "ordinary and usual" meaning and usually interpret the meaning against the drafter. If the writer is unable to define the term, potential offerors will have the same difficulty.

j. Avoid using "any," "either," or "and/or" unless you want to give the contractor a choice in what must be done. Also, avoid the use of "etc.," because the reader doesn't have any idea of the items that could be missing.

k. Include definitions that provide a common basis for understanding between the contractor doing the work for you. Ensure each "term of art" has only one universally understood meaning; otherwise define it.

l. Use abbreviations or acronyms only after spelling them out the first time they are referenced. When there are many, it is advisable to provide an appendix.

m. Any document referenced in the solicitation must be either furnished with the solicitation or available at a location identified in the solicitation. The date or version of each document must also be specified, not listed as "version in effect on date of award."

n. Do not duplicate material in the PWS or SOW that the chief contracting officer will include in other parts of the contract/solicitation. Consult the chief procurement officer for guidance during the early stages of PWS or SOW preparation.

o. As part of the initial proposal, offerors can (1) be required to submit detailed plans for compliance with Safety and Health Requirements, Quality System and Assurance Requirements, and similar items, or (2) allowed to submit summary plans accompanied by a statement to provide more detailed plans if selected. A preference must be stated in the Purchase Request package.

p. The Project Manager should indicate, if appropriate, desired design output, verification, and how design changes will be managed. The inspection portion shall address inspection and testing requirements (if appropriate, reference ISO elements). It may be helpful to have the contractor develop a quality plan or documented procedure that will be used to inspect and test the product or identify non-conforming items. If appropriate, reference ISO elements for Design and for Process Control.

q. In all cases, performance work statements and even statements of work must:

(1) be definitive enough to protect the your interests if you are the buyer;

(2) serve as a basis for contractor response, evaluation of proposals, and source selection; and

(3) provide a meaningful measure of performance so both the you and the contractor will know when the work is satisfactorily completed (see Appendix D).

Deliverables

a. This section contains information on what the contractor/vendor is required to provide and when it is required. Identify only those outputs that are essential and a part of the performance requirement's summary. Express the outputs in concise, easily understood, measurable terms.

b. Clearly state which party will perform each task by delineating a division of responsibilities between you they buyer, the contractor, and others.

(1) If review is to be provided by government or a commercial buyer, a time limit must be set within which review/comment must be provided. Each time the contractor suspends activity to wait for a response, time and money are expended. To avoid a breach of contract by the Government, the contract should state "*the contractor shall presume "no comment" and proceed if comment is not provided within _____*" (a specified period).

(2) Clauses or statements that make contractor performance dependent on the government or a commercial buyer must be avoided. A contract shall clearly state the intended effect of interim reviews to

avoid releasing the contractor from subsequent liability. For example, if the contractor's overall obligation is to design and build an item that meets a final specification but a review of the design is

required before proceeding, such review should not be considered as an approval. Courts have generally held that an approval transfers responsibility to the approving party. Beware of the contractor giving accountability back to the party buying a product or service while they are being paid to be accountable. A contractor may readily agree or even request your review and approval of their plans and procedures. **Do not do it!** You need to make the supplier of goods or services accountable for their work outputs and or deliverables.

c. Provide a realistic delivery schedule for contract performance and completion. Schedules that are unnecessarily short or difficult to attain tend to restrict competition and result in higher contract prices. Provide sufficient information for the contractor to establish its own milestones against which its progress can be measured. Be sure this section is consistent with the rest of the solicitation.

Data Requirements

a. Minimize the data requirements because asking for data costs money. Buy only the data needed to make a decision and/or comply with a higher level requirement. Reduce costs by requesting data that will normally be created in performance of the contract. Avoid contractor proprietary information management or technical data systems that hinder oversight or create a sole source problem in follow-on procurements. Don't request reports that can generate on it's own from contractor data.

b. The Purchase Request Initiator must prepare a list of all data to be delivered under the contract, including the time and frequency of delivery. This includes information on the status of the contractor effort, information needed to support, manage, and operate the system, and using contractor formats or those common to the contractor's customers, if feasible.

c. In major system acquisitions, all data requirements must be specified in a separate line item listed in a section of the solicitation other than the PWS.

Use of Property

a. In the federal government, the FAR requires that contractors provide all facilities required for performance of government contracts unless the contracting situation falls within one of the stated exceptions. Facilities used in this context refers to real property (i.e., land, buildings, and other structures) and plant equipment (i.e., general purpose equipment, test equipment, furniture, computers, vehicles, and similar items). The same rule applies to furnishing material, except the government may do so to achieve significant economy or standardization, or when in the government's interest.

b. Providing equipment to contractors on-site must be done sparingly since the contractor will be dependent upon the government for care and maintenance. This dependence may hinder the ability of contractors to be fully accountable. It is best to make contractors fully responsible for owning or renting whatever equipment or property they need. Never involve the government.

c. When furnishing government property to contractors appears necessary, care must be taken to assure that regulatory authority exists and that appropriate documentation is prepared justifying an exception to general policy. Following this determination, the identification of each item, time of delivery, and condition (if feasible) of the government property must be itemized. It's a lot of work and time that simply is not needed.

PROTECTING THE INTEGRITY OF THE PROCESS

The acquisition process must be conducted in a manner above reproach, with complete impartiality and with no preferential treatment to make your procurement and ethical one with strong integrity. All personnel associated with the acquisition process have a responsibility to protect its integrity:

> (1)All potential offerors must be given equal access to information on competitive acquisitions. Generally draft Requests for Proposals (RFPs), pre-solicitation/ pre-proposal conferences, and/or one-on-one discussions between purchasing technical personnel and potential offerors improve the acquisition process. However, any information that could give an offeror a competitive advantage must be made available to all potential offerors.
> (2) In the interval between release of a competitive solicitation and contract award, all communication with prospective contractors relating to the acquisition must be through the Contracting Officer.
> (3) Proprietary and source selection sensitive information must be protected from unauthorized disclosure.
> (4) Specifications, PWS and SOWs must not be unnecessarily restrictive to avoid unfairly excluding one vendor or increasing prospects for award to another.
> (5) Contractors that prepare YOUR PWS or SOWs are generally prohibited from proposing on that...it is an organizational conflict of interest.

KEY PARTICIPANTS

The organization needing contractor support is required to provide the PWS or Specification; however, writing these documents must always be a team effort. The Project Manager and the Contracting Officer or Commercial Purchasing Manager will build a team that includes personnel who are experts in the technical disciplines, financial management, fabrication, test, logistics, configuration management, operations, safety, reliability, maintainability, and quality assurance. Contractor personnel or consultants cannot be members of this team without written justification by the appropriate Chief of Procurement.

Project Manager

The requesting organization will assign an individual who is familiar with the technical requirements of the procurement to be responsible for writing the PWS/SOW. This person will define and articulate the contract requirements and is also responsible for planning, program control functions, developing program objectives, delivery requirements, scheduling, estimating, budgeting, specific project plans, surveillance plan development, and participating in the source selection.

Contracting Officer or Chief Commercial Buyer

Contracting Officers or Commercial Purchasing Managers are responsible for ensuring performance of the contract, and safeguarding the interest of the agency or firm's contractual relationships. The CO or Chief Purchasing Officer does not decide the need, but rather assists the project manager in preparation of a PWS/SOW/specification that clearly states agency or firm's needs in conformance with the regulations. A CO or Chief Purchaser is the only member of the team that has authority to obligate funds.

Contracting Officer's Representative (COR)

The technical Program Office will nominate as COR which acts as a agent for "the government" who is an employee with the technical expertise necessary to administer the contract. This person must have received training, and is often the Project Manager who initiated the Procurement Request (PR). At contract award, the CO or Chief Buyers will issue a letter of delegation that specifies the limits of the COR's authority. This appointment enables the COR to assist the CO or Chief Buyers with the technical aspects of the contract. Generally Commercial Purchasing Managers do not have similar positions.

Quality Assurance Representative (QAR)

The QAR provides the quality assurance requirements, and assists in developing performance standards and project surveillance plans. The QAR is also responsible for evaluating contractor performance in accordance with the pre-established Surveillance Plan.

CHAPTER 3
REQUIREMENTS ANALYSIS

GETTING STARTED

Requirements analysis determines what YOUR needs are, and what kinds of services and outputs are to be provided by a contractor. A systematic process for PWS/SOW development begins with an analysis of what work is to be performed and breaks down the work into components. It ends with a clear description of performance output requirements.

WORK BREAKDOWN STRUCTURES (WBS)

a. The WBS is a top-level overview that provides the basis for monitoring a program or project by subdividing the work into successively smaller increments until a manageable element is reached. It develops a program-team consensus on what the customer wants. Together with a make/buy determination, it can be a useful tool in deciding what elements are performed by civil servants and by contractors. A good WBS assures that significant tasks are not overlooked.

b. Although the WBS can be a valuable tool, it is not necessary for all procurements. When used, the WBS must avoid stifling innovative ideas. Rigid control of every detail is neither necessary nor desirable. It must not be so explicit that there is no room for creative thinking or individual empowerment, yet it must be sufficiently defined and all work elements identified to permit inspection and acceptance.

GATHERING HISTORICAL DATA

a. After identification by means of the WBS of services or products that are required, resource data are gathered for both in-house and contractor efforts. This involves collecting and analyzing historical data (indicating what, when, how much, etc. relative to prior work performed) to describe the job, establish how often the service or output is needed, and ensure that we don't pay for something that has already been done. Then define objectives or goals that differentiate the programs. Finally, establish a historical background of prior successes/failures throughout this program.

b. Data required is available from internal and external databases or records (such as sampling or on-the-job observations), or from other agencies and businesses that have acquired similar products or services. Also, where applicable, review past safety violations, OSHA judgments, EPA violations or citations, and employee lost-time accident rates.

Benchmarking

The purpose of benchmarking is to improve the workings of your own organization by taking advantage of another organization's Lessons Learned and to avoid mistakes made in the past. In the early steps of planning, communicate with other organizations to gain insight on similar requirements. Then follow the four basic steps to benchmarking: preparation, observation, comparison, and action.

(1) Preparation means identifying contracts similar to the one you are trying to write, but do not limit your search to just government contracts, use any many different and other commercial contracts as possible. Networking at procurement offices can often lead to other connections. Be prepared with specific questions concerning expected deliverables, services, etc., and what measures they use in determining success.

(2) The second and most important step is observation. Write down all facts that are useful. Find out what the organization has learned both good and bad. Observe how successful its approach has been. You could also request a copy of their PWS to use as a template.

(3) The third phase is comparison. Look at the information gained and ask, "what useful and relevant information did I get?" Make a matrix of what is needed and what you got to assist in understanding how to apply the information received.

(4) The final phase is action. Now apply what was learned by drafting the PWS. Continue working with procurement, your technical staff, and other

managers so problem areas and missing details can be identified. You may want to have one of the benchmarking organizations help you, but be careful since you may be in a procurement-sensitive phase.

Output Data

One of the most important and difficult tasks of the team is to find how often output services will be furnished during contract performance. Historical information must be modified by incorporating anticipated changes. In Performance-Based Contracting this information may be made available to the contractor for information purposes only.

Physical Resources Data

Another challenging task is to gather data on facilities, materials, and equipment required to support the work to be performed. As a general rule, contractors are required to provide all resources for work they will be doing for your firm or an agency. However, in the rare exceptions where equipment is furnished to them (rare), writers of the PWS will use the resources data to develop their list of Government-furnished property.

Personnel Resources Data

Gather data on the numbers and types of personnel that may be needed to perform each service output. This will be useful in evaluating a proposal's cost realism and in developing the Government estimate. It is the responsibility of the contractor to manage its own staffing plan. This gives the contractor latitude to manage its own work force and choose its own methods for work accomplishment. The contract should not normally specify staffing levels or use "key personnel" clauses.

Quality Systems Data

Data on the contractor's ability to meet contract requirements should be in accordance with ISO 9000 standards; including quality system and QA requirements.

PROJECT WORK BREAKDOWN STRUCTURES (PWBS)

a. The WBS will be further developed from the program level downward to a project-by-project basis by means of the PWBS. A PWBS is prepared when project definition permits and will be refined and changed as design concepts change to reflect new system and subsystem approaches. Until a project is completed, the PWBS is a flexible working tool.

(1) It includes all effort required to achieve an end objective. It encompasses total project content by relating the elements of work to each other and to the end product. A PWBS, which describes inputs, covers both in-house and contractor efforts.

(2) It is developed by displaying and defining the total effort to be performed in identifiable and measurable elements. A PWBS element can represent varying aggregations of individual jobs or tasks, each of which is planned, approved, and managed at an appropriate level. No task should be overlooked.

(3) It provides the framework for project planning and control and also for making decisions conducive to effective use of contractor support.

(4) It provides means for integrating and assessing technical, schedule, and cost performance.

(5) It provides a framework for performance measurement.

(6) It provides all applicable quality systems and quality assurance requirements, as well as definition of the type and extent of control to be exercised on subcontracts.

(7) All element descriptions are concise and easy to understand.

b. A PWBS must also be compatible with the coding structure defined for your organizations accounting and financial systems of collecting data.

c. Following a PWBS breakdown, the section of the PWBS identifying contracting efforts is extended by using a contract WBS (CWBS).

CONTRACT WORK BREAKDOWN STRUCTURES (CWBS).

a. For non-routine, more complex requirements, a CWBS is created. A CWBS is a hierarchical diagram for a specific contract. It identifies the requirements to be satisfied, **leaving the contractor free to determine how to achieve the desired result**.

b. A CWBS is prepared prior to writing the PWS and serves as an "outline" for the technical requirements contained in the PWS. A good CWBS makes a PWS easier to write, facilitates preparation of contractor proposals, helps in preparation of the in-house estimate, and assists with evaluation and source selection activities.

(1) The first step is to provide a systematic approach to facilitate project management by breaking the effort into easily managed units of work that have an identifiable output and a similar technical or managerial nature. Divide the overall requirement into major phases or tasks that represent a logical, and usually chronological, division of the work effort.

(2) For the second step, the major tasks required to achieve the end objectives are identified.

(3) Then, in the third and final step, each task is broken down further into sub-phases; normally to no more than three levels of detail. Remember, each level identified by the Government in the PWS will limit the innovation and creativity allowed to the contractor on that level. In addition, avoid developing the PWBS to a level so low that it will be in conflict with industry's normal management practices.

(4) When complete, the CWBS will break down each component, when the primary end item is hardware, as follows:

FUNCTONS REQUIRED	Levels
1. Contract, Space Shuttle System	**I**
1.1 Propulsion System	**II**
1.1.1 Fan	**III**
1.1.2 Compressor	
1.1.3 Turbine	
1.2 Guidance	
1.3 Life Support System	
1.4 Project Management	
1.4.1 Performance Reports	

Note: Changes to the CWBS recommended by the contractor should be examined. In the above chart, a choice was made by launching agency to go down to three levels. This is true of most organizations such as Lockheed Martin, Northrup Gruman, and other large fortune 100 OEMs or integrators.

Remember, this limits the contractor in proposing any innovative methods in lieu of what is required in those three levels.

Extension of the CWBS by Contractors

a. In the RFP, contractors will be instructed to include in their proposals an extension of the CWBS to a level compatible with their management systems, e.g., earned value reporting.
b. The proposals normally include:

> (1) **A Configuration Item** that is an aggregation of all the hardware and computer programs or any of its discrete portions, which satisfies an end-use function and is designated by the agency for configuration management. They may vary widely in complexity, size, and type. During development and manufacture of the initial (prototype) production configuration, they are those specification items whose functions and performance parameters must be defined and controlled to achieve the overall end-use function and performance. An item required for logistic support and designated for separate procurement is a configuration item.

> (2) **High Risk Items** that involve technological, manufacturing or other state-of-the-art advances or considerations. They are critical in achieving program objectives, reliability, maintainability, safety, quality assurance or other such factors. They are designated

by program/project management as requiring special attention.

(3) **Major Subcontracts and Inter-divisional Work** that are identified at the appropriate level on the extended CWBS. If they are large or complex enough, they are broken down to the same extent as if the tasks were a prime contract.

(4) **Cost Accounts** that are clear definitions of work to be performed and are distinct from other cost accounts. They have measurable beginning and end points.

c. Whenever Contractor Financial Management Reporting is required, all reporting categories must correlate with the CWBS as well as with the contractor's own accounting system. In addition, each CWBS shall be designed to facilitate accounting for costs in accordance with the Agency-wide Coding Structure found in most Financial Management policy requirements.

d. The extended CWBS will help in evaluating the contractor's understanding of the work to be done and of cost realism.

Contractual Use of the CWBS

a. The CWBS may be changed during negotiations to meet the needs of the Purchaser and/or the contractor. In routine efforts, it becomes the basis, in conjunction with the PWS, against which the contractor performs the effort. In non-routine efforts, the CWBS should be a flexible guide developed by and for the use of the contractor, but the acceptance of the product should be against the performance standards.

b. Upon award, the levels of the CWBS that become part of the contract are what have been agreed upon by both parties; this is usually the top three levels. At that point, the CWBS cannot be changed except by modification of that contract.

PURCHASER COST ESTIMATES

a. Preparation of an estimate of costs to perform the effort is a responsibility of the Project Manager for the purchasing activity, with support from other technical experts and budgetary personnel. Estimated costs for each service output, based on available data, include details of assumptions made in preparing the estimate. These costs are also used in evaluating proposals and determining positive and negative performance incentives. The level of documentation required is dependent on the complexity and dollar value of the procurement. For major acquisitions, an independent cost estimate is often required.

b. Government agencies mostly opt for integrated full cost accounting, budgeting and management changes and practices to optimize the anticipated cost effective mission benefits of its full cost initiative. Full cost accounting is required by Federal legislation and related guidance. Full cost budgeting and management are indicated in Federal legislation and related guidance but are not always specifically required. With commercial purchasers accounting is more optional. The strength and benefits of full cost practices are optimized by the integration and synergy of changes in each area. Full cost accounting by itself, over time, would likely lead to gradual budget and management improvements. However, concurrent changes to full cost practices in the accounting, budgeting and management areas can be expected to ensure that an agency or organization will optimize improvements in each area immediately.

c. Agencies must also consider commercial costs of performing similar work in the private sector.

d. In-house cost estimates (labor hours, material costs, software requirements, etc.) developed by the cost estimating specialists must be reviewed by PWS contributors. Such reviews will permit early trade-off consideration on the desirability of requirements that are not directly related to essential technical objectives. These estimates will also be used to assist evaluators in determining if proposal costs are realistic.

CHAPTER 4
PERFORMANCE WORK STATEMENTS (PWS)

GENERAL

Performance-Based Contracting means structuring all aspects of an acquisition around the purpose of the work to be performed - <u>not to dictate how the work is to be accomplished</u>. It is designed to ensure that contractors be given the freedom to determine how to meet contract performance objectives, the appropriate performance levels are achieved, and that payment is only made for results that meet these levels. It maximizes contractor control of work processes and allows for innovation in approaching various work requirements. Remember, when vendors (contractors) are not told "how" to do the job, their ingenuity may surprise you.

Performance-Based Contracting emphasizes performance that can be contractually defined so that the results of the contractor's effort can be measured in terms of technical and quality achievement, schedule progress, or cost performance. The significant steps in the PBC process include:

> (1) emphasizing contract performance requirements that can be measured by a meaningful performance evaluation;
>
> (2) selecting contractors that provide "best value" with proven past performance;
>
> (3) providing positive incentives for good performance;
>
> (4) determining contract type and incentives in accordance with a fair assessment and assignment of

performance risk;

(5) performing contract surveillance and administration for insight only into essential areas of contractor performance; and

(6) being mindful of the need for conservation of resources.

The goal of PBC is to:

(1) Save money by reducing contract costs by eliminating unnecessary effort and through innovation by the contractor, and also by reducing purchaser surveillance.

(2) Enable purchasers to shift its emphasis from processes to outputs.

(3) Hold contractors (suppliers) accountable for the end results (outputs).

(4) Ensure that contractors (suppliers) are given the freedom to determine how to meet the Purchaser's performance objectives.

c. The following decision tree must be used by those who draft requirement documents.

PBC Roadmap

Can the purchaser assign performance responsibility to the contractor (supplier), and can performance be validated against a performance standard?	**Yes>**	**Write a performance-based contract**
If No--		
Can discrete portions of the effort be assigned to the contractor for performance responsibility, and can performance against those portions be validated against performance standards?	**Yes>**	**Specify performance standards in the contract.**
If No--		
Specify critical processes in the contract or contract-referenced documents.		

To be considered PBC, a PWS must include meaningful measurable performance standards and the quality level the purchaser expects the contractor to provide. There are two categories of PBC-type contracts: contracts of a routine nature and contracts of a non-routine nature.

Routine Services

a. In contracting for services of a routine nature, whether high or low "tech" (e.g., computer service, guard service, or janitorial), it is essential to avoid under-specifying requirements. Work inadvertently omitted may later be construed to be outside the requirements (outside the contractual scope of work) for the contract and could require a contract change and increased costs. Even worse, omissions outside the scope of the contract could require a significant effort from the purchaser; a new competition or a Justification for use of something other than open competition.

b. The PWS for routine services is usually written to require **output** (see Appendix D). In the absence of a performance-based standard, a purchaser may not be able to ensure that the contractor completes the work at an acceptable level. In that event, the purchaser may be obligated to accept whatever product or service the contractor provides or make changes in the work requirements and pay more to acquire what is actually needed.

c. There is usually a significant amount of data available for routine services plus a competitive marketplace with several suppliers; consequently, a firm-fixed price contract with deduction schedules (which are applied when performance is inadequate) is commonly used.

Non-Routine Requirements

When acquiring supplies, engineering, or unique non-routine services (including studies, analyses, or R&D efforts), performance-based specifications must **avoid over-specifying (or gold-plating)** purchaser requirements. Accordingly, the PWS for non-routine work is usually written to require an **outcome** (see Appendix D). The policy limits the involvement of purchaser employees and provides contractors (suppliers) the maximum flexibility in meeting YOUR need. If that need is succinctly defined, the contractor should be entrusted to fulfill that need.

GUIDELINES FOR WRITING A PWS

a. The contract will be a completion form (something is accomplished) as opposed to a term/level-of-effort form.

b. To the maximum extent practicable (FAR Part 11.002), state the requirements in terms of:

(1) Functions to be performed;
(2) Performance required; or

> **The PWS must include performance requirements and verification requirements that are measurable or quantifiable.**

c. Without specifying how to perform the work, the PWS must clearly indicate the expected outcomes or outputs from the contractor such that contractor performance can be measured against the performance standards in the PWS. The definitions of standard performance, maximum positive and negative performance incentives, and the units of measurement will be established in the solicitation. They will vary from contract to contract and are subject to discussion during source selection.

d. To aid in continuity and to avoid confusion, the PWS format must conform to the numerical coding of the related task elements of the CWBS). The coded task descriptions clearly define each deliverable end item, product, and task.

Hardware or End Item Deliverables

The PWS or specification describes, at the highest practicable level, what the end product must do (performance) and any critical constraints (e.g., size, weight). It eliminates process-oriented (how to) requirements and includes only minimally essential reporting requirements. The contract requirements and incentives are clearly communicated. Actual demonstrated performance of the end item is normally one of the measures -- in some cases the only measure.

Performance Based Specification

a. A major effect of acquisition reform is that the number of performance statements should be increased and the number of detailed, design-solution statements should be decreased over time. A performance specification, which shall be used to the greatest extent practicable, describes the work broadly by *form, fit, and function* instead of using detailed drawings, specifications, and standards which can be flawed. Offerors (suppliers) are free to meet the requirements in any way they can. This increases the purchaser's access to commercial, state-of-the-art technology. Requirements are expressed in terms of minimum acceptable performance standards known as AQLs or Acceptable Quality Levels (see Appendix E) and place maximum responsibility for performance on the contractor or supplier. Additional information, such as standards, may be referenced as information to providers to improve understanding, but should be clearly separated from requirements.

b. A performance specification also requires results, with criteria for verifying compliance without stating methods for achieving the required results. By not specifying an approach in manufacturing, design, or quality assurance to be used by the contractor, it permits a wide variety of contractor methods; thereby potentially increasing the number of contractors who can satisfy the requirement. Contractors (suppliers) can use their creative and innovative skills to the maximum.

c. Nevertheless, PBC emphasis does not preclude highly descriptive specifications, which (if expressed in performance terms) accurately and inclusively describe what we want done or delivered.

d. In writing performance-based specifications, avoid the following:

>(1) Performance specified at the subsystem or component level when it could be more appropriately specified at a higher level; e.g., the reliability of the system or vehicle should be specified instead of specific components with the system.
>
>(2) Requirements that are not measurable or verifiable.
>
>(3) Statements that constrain the solution to a single solution; e.g., "shall be fabricated from composite material."
>
>(4) Orphan requirements; i.e., requirement statements that are not traceable to a specific performance or verification requirement statement in the specification.

(5) Requirement statements that are not appropriate for an effort in this phase of development or production.

(6) Specifications relying solely on directives to define performance, not the mission requirements.

(7) Citing standards and processes when performance standards can be developed.

(8) Citing of mandatory standards without justification.

(9) Requirements that are vague (e.g., "in accordance with commercial practices" in lieu of citing a commercial standard).

(10) Language in the specification that belongs in the PWS.

e. Listed below are key elements to be considered in preparing specifications and the related technical requirements.

(1) Description of supplies, or data that identifies the requirement. When appropriate, describe requirements broadly by form, fit, and function.

(2) Quantity (and unit).

(3) Packaging and marking requirements.

(4) Inspection, acceptance, and quality assurance. The concern for quality must be expressed by providing standards which result in proposals that offer credible responses concerning the ability to perform quality work; e.g., if the surface must not

contain imperfections exceeding .01 inch, specifically state this as the assessment of quality.

(5) Place of delivery, performance and delivery dates, period of performance, and f.o.b. point. Efforts shall be made to give prospective contractors adequate time to produce the item or to provide the required service.

(6) Other information as necessary.

Systems Contracts

a. Contracts for definition and development of "Systems" have short, concise outcome PWS documents that do not necessarily go into great detail. There is usually a specification/contract deliverable requirements list associated with these contracts, which may contain specific requirements for the product(s). The PWS must, however, state all requirements necessary to complete each task element of the WBS and be complete enough to allow the contractor to generate all information necessary to design, prototype, test, and verify.

b. A good approach for the acquisition of systems is to acquire the effort in phases, with each phase having a limited but clear objective. This approach also is a safeguard against committing scarce resources to an effort prematurely.

c. For study and preliminary definition contracts, the PWS must allow the contractor wide latitude for creativity, innovation and research. Describe efforts necessary to supplement existing information and bring present knowledge to a point where further detailed study for the most promising systems can be made.

Support Services

The PWS generally describe all of the services to be performed and includes explicit, measurable performance standards, surveillance procedures, and incentives. It includes only minimally essential reporting requirements, but the contractor will be held accountable for failure to meet those minimum requirements. **The outline will be similar to the following:**

1. Introduction
2. Scope of Work
3. Management or Administration
4. Description of Work or Services
4.1 Performance Standards Required
4.2 Performance Requirements Summary (PRS)
5. Contract Deliverables to be supplied
6. Essential Reports Required
7. Appendices
8. Special Terms and Conditions

In preparing a PWS or a task assignment consider the following:

a. The PWS clearly describes the specific requirements the contractor is required to meet in performance of the contract. Specify the minimum required level of performance and quality, failing which, the objective of the contract or task will not be met.

b. Over-defining the contractor's responsibilities in terms of methods or procedures must be avoided since the

Government is purchasing a result/service or some requirement which includes not only the contractor's labor, but also its expertise in the services to be provided and the management of those services. Place the responsibility for success on the contractor (supplier), not the purchaser or agency.

c. On the other hand, provide enough information to define clearly and precisely the magnitude and complexity of the outcome/output desired. This will slightly restrict the contractor in managing their work force, but will help ensure all bidders clearly visualize the extent of effort required.

d. In addition to the desired outputs or outcomes:

> (1) specify the schedules of accomplishment and/or time limitations in which all services must be completed,
>
> (2) provide a list of mandatory operating and safety procedures that the contractor must follow, and
>
> (3) provide historical data on previous contracts or work by in-house personnel. This needs to be done carefully to avoid specifying staffing levels, etc.

e. In those cases where the Purchaser can provide only a broad description, use of a task order contract shall be considered. Individual task orders can be written that clearly define each deliverable end item or product and include performance standards and incentives. All essential tasks must be included.

Research and Development (R&D) Contracts

a. Unlike contracts for supplies and services, most R&D contracts are directed toward specified objectives and knowledge where the work or methods cannot be precisely described in advance. It is difficult to judge the probabilities of ultimate success or required effort for technical approaches. R&D PWSs can be difficult to write if the contract's objectives are not defined sufficiently, yet they must be flexible enough to allow contractors freedom to exercise innovation and creativity. The most important performance-based element is to clearly define the requirements and/or the schedule such that the performance of the contractor is measurable. Following is a sample outline:

1. Introduction
2. Scope of Work or Services
3. Description of Tasks to Be Performed (Desired Outputs)
4. Delivery Schedule
5. Reports Required
6. Attachments, Appendices and Exhibits

b. Typically for R&D, the contractor has a cost-type contract, therefore, has no cost risk for the supplier. However, if the contractor receives a small fee for performing "best efforts," the substantive portion of any fee must be tied to successful performance - an objective measurement is preferred, however, at times a subjective determination could be meaningful and acceptable.

Basic Research

a. In basic research results cannot be determined in advance and often no deliverable is required except for a final report. In that case, the performance standards may be focused on timeliness, organization and thoroughness of the report, comprehensive bibliography, etc. These performance standards shall be used to "gate" contractor eligibility for fee, if any.

b. When the principle purpose of the research is for the direct benefit or use of purchaser's organization, a contract shall always be created.

APPENDIX A
DOCUMENT REVIEW CHECKLIST

The following Checklist should be reviewed prior to forwarding the PWS/specification for approval. It is a guide only, and items should be added or deleted to tailor it to the specific document.

1. Can I give the contractor (supplier) full management responsibility and hold them accountable for the end results? Can I perform a meaningful evaluation of performance? Does my draft PWS reflect this strategy?
2. Is the PWS sufficiently detailed to permit both the agency purchaser and the contractor (supplier) to estimate costs, to tabulate labor and other resources required to accomplish each task element? Will the contractors be able to prepare a sound technical and cost proposal?
3. Are standards clear that make it possible for all parties to measure performance?
4. Is the PWS/specification too restrictive? Does it tell contractors how to run their business?
5. Are proper quantities and delivery dates indicated for each deliverable?
6. When necessary to reference other documents, is the proper reference document described and cited? Is the entire document pertinent to the task or should only portions be referenced? Is it cross-referenced to the applicable PWS task element?
7. Have all requirements for data been specified separately in a Data Requirements Listing section? Have all extraneous data requirements been eliminated? Are requirements specified adequately to obtain sufficient data to permit competition for anticipated follow-on procurements? Have appropriate agency purchaser and industry standards been researched and referenced in the PWS, as necessary? Have requirements to use

agency standards been limited to those where it is impractical to use non-agency standards8.Are all safety, reliability, quality assurance, and security requirements defined for the total life of the contract?
8. Has extraneous material been eliminated?
9. Has the document been checked for format and grammar? Are subheadings compatible with the subject matter of the heading? Is the text compatible with the title? Is a multi-decimal or alpha-numeric numbering system used in the PWS that can be cross-referenced to the CWBS?
10. Are all terms used consistently throughout, and adequately defined, including "industry-wide" terms?
11. Does the PWS cover the requirements imposed on the contractor's (supplier's) quality system to ensure that products conform to requirements?
12. Does the PWS cover any design or process control requirements required by the purchaser? Does the PWS cover any specific purchaser requirements for inspection and testing?
13. Does the PWS provide for corrective/preventive action by the contractor in the event the product delivered is non-conforming to the specified product?

APPENDIX B
DEFINITIONS

CONTRACT--A bilateral agreement between two or more parties, enforceable by law, that obligates the seller to furnish something, and obligates the buyer to pay for it.

COST-PLUS-AWARD-FEE CONTRACT (CPAF)--A cost-reimbursement contract that provides for a fee consisting of an award amount, based upon a judgmental evaluation by the Government, sufficient to provide motivation for excellence in contract performance.

COST-PLUS-INCENTIVE-FEE CONTRACT (CPIF) A cost-reimbursement contract that provides for the initially negotiated fee to be adjusted later by a formula based on the relationship of total allowable costs to total target costs. The contract may include technical performance incentives when it is highly probable that the required development of a program is feasible and the Government has established its performance objectives.

COST-REIMBURSEMENT CONTRACT--A type of contract that provides for payment of allowable incurred costs, to the extent prescribed in the contract. These contracts establish an estimate of total costs for the purpose of obligating funds and establishing a ceiling that the contractor may not exceed without approval of the CO.

FEDERAL ACQUISITION REGULATION (FAR)--The Federal regulation that implements procurement-related statutes and governs Government procurement.

FIXED-PRICE CONTRACT--A contract where the contractor agrees to deliver supplies or services at the times specified for an agreed upon price that cannot be changed unless the Government modifies the contract.

SYSTEM ACQUISITION--Those programs that are directed at and critical to fulfilling an agency's mission, entail the allocation of relatively large resources, and warrant special management attention.

NEGOTIATIONS--Written or oral discussions usually conducted with the selected offeror(s) to settle cost and other terms, which will be incorporated into the resultant contract.

OBJECTIVE PERFORMANCE MEASURE--Based on the attributes of physical objects that can be measured or counted.

OFFER--A response to a solicitation that, if accepted, would bind the offeror to perform the resultant contract. Responses to invitations for bids (sealed bidding) are offers called "bids" or "sealed bids." Responses to requests for proposals (negotiation) are offers called "proposals."

OUTCOME MEASURE--An assessment of the results of a program activity compared to its intended purpose (objective).

OUTPUT MEASURE--The tabulation, calculation, or recording of activity or effort and can be expressed in a quantitative or qualitative manner.

PERFORMANCE-BASED CONTRACTING--Structuring all aspects of an acquisition around the purpose of the work to be performed as opposed to either the manner by which the work is to be performed or broad and imprecise statements of work.

PROPOSAL--A response by a prospective contractor (supplier) to a Purchaser's Request for Proposals issued by the CO or Purchasing Official in negotiated acquisitions. It is an offer (including technical performance, as well as cost or price terms) that can be accepted to create a binding contract, either following negotiations or when certain conditions are satisfied. The term "bid" is used in sealed bid procurements.

PROPOSAL EVALUATION FACTORS--Factors against which proposals are evaluated. The RFP must explain these factors and their order of importance.

PURCHASE OR PROCUREMENT REQUEST (PR)--The document prepared by the requiring activity which (1) describes the supplies or services to be acquired, (2) certifies the availability of funds, and (3) includes other information and approvals necessary to initiate an acquisition action.

REASONABLE COST--A cost which in its nature and amount does not exceed that which would be incurred by a prudent person in the conduct of competitive business. If challenged, the burden of proof for determining cost reasonableness rests with the contractor.

REQUEST FOR PROPOSALS (RFP)--The Government's invitation (solicitation) to prospective offerors to submit proposals based on the terms and conditions set forth in a RFP.

SERVICES--The performance of identifiable tasks rather than the delivery of an end item of supply. Services also include tasks that are delivered under a contract where the primary purpose of the contract is to provide supplies.

SOLE SOURCE CONTRACT--A contract awarded as a result of a solicitation that was provided to only one offeror or as a result of an unsolicited proposal.

SOLICITATION--A formal invitation by the Government to prospective offerors to submit offers to satisfy a purchasing agency's need. It describes the requirements in sufficient detail to allow prospective offerors to determine their ability to meet that need and to submit a meaningful offer. It also includes the terms, conditions, and instructions under which offers may be submitted and resultant contracts will be awarded.

STATEMENT OF WORK (SOW)-- A tasking document that specifies effort to be performed by a contractor.

SURVEILLANCE: The continual monitoring and verification of status of an entity and analysis of records to ensure specified requirements are being met. Surveillance activities may be delegated to other disinterested parties on behalf of the customer. It may be 100%, statistically-based sampling, qualitative sampling, or the result of discussion with individuals who have first-hand knowledge. It also may include the monitoring of contractor supplied metrics, available contractor data, sampling, or surveys.

TECHNICAL EVALUATION-- The measurement of a technical proposal against the technical requirements and the rating factors stated in the solicitation. Cost may be considered as an indicator of understanding of technical requirements.

TECHNICAL STANDARD-- common and repeated use of rules, conditions, guidelines or characteristics for products or related processes and production methods. It includes the definition of terms, classification of components, delineation of procedures, specification of dimensions, materials, performance, designs, or operations. It includes measurement of quality and quantity as well as a description of fit and measurements.

WORK BREAKDOWN STRUCTURE (WBS). A product-oriented, hierarchical division tree of deliverable items and associated services that relates the elements of work to each other and to the end item.

APPENDIX C
ACRONYM LIST

CO	Contracting Officer
COR	Contracting Officer's Representative
CWBS	Contract Work Breakdown Structure
FAR	Federal Acquisition Regulation
NFS	NASA FAR Supplement
OMB	Office of Management and Budget
PBC	Performance-Based Contracting
PR	Purchase or Procurement Request
PWBS	Project Work Breakdown Structure
PWS	Performance Work Statement
QR	Quality Representative
RFP	Requests for Proposals
R&D	Research and Development
SOW	Statement of Work
WBS	Work Breakdown Schedule

APPENDIX D
PBC PERFORMANCE STANDARDS AND INCENTIVES

INTRODUCTION

a. **A PBC must contain performance standards** -- the criteria for determining whether the work requirements are met. A performance standard must be assigned to essential or critical (but not incidental) tasks or products.

b. A baseline is established from which continuous improvement will be sought over the life of the contract, and is composed of three elements:

> (1) **Outcome or Output.** The desired result, or necessary effort, being acquired
>
> (2) **Performance Standard.** The measurement threshold or limit that establishes that point at which successful performance has been accomplished.
>
> (3) **Surveillance.** The monitoring and verification of performance.

OUTCOME OR OUTPUT

a. An **outcome** measure is an assessment of the results of a program activity compared to its intended purpose. An outcome-based contract is often ideal for non-routine efforts.

b. An **output** measure is the tabulation, calculation, or recording of activity or effort and can be expressed in a quantitative or qualitative manner. For routine efforts an output contract may be more desirable.

c. Describe the outcome/output but do not give specific procedures or instructions on how to produce them unless absolutely necessary. When a purchasing organization specifies a procedure (how to do it), purchasing organization assumes responsibility for ensuring that the design or procedure will end with the desired result. However, if purchasing organization specifies the outcome/output performance and its quality standard, the contractor must then use its best judgment in determining how to achieve that level of performance. A key tenet of PBC is that the supplier will be assigned the responsibility to meet the purchasing organization's requirements together with the flexibility to decide how it will meet those needs. The purchasing organization then evaluates the contractor's performance against the standard. In many cases, the final arrangement can be a hybrid contract with a limited number of critical specifications being imposed on the contractor.

PERFORMANCE STANDARDS

a. Explicit, measurable performance standards must be included in the PWS or specification for a contract to be considered performance based. Under PBC, the purchasing organization expresses its willingness to accept the contractor solution as long as it meets performance requirements.

b. A Performance Standard states requirements in terms of required results, with criteria for verifying compliance but without stating the methods for achieving required results. It defines the requirements for the item and/or services, the environment in which it must operate, and interface and interchangeability characteristics. Performance standards must be:

(1) Meaningful. An objective measurement is preferred, however, at times a subjective determination could be meaningful and acceptable.

(2) Understandable, and clearly communicated to the contractor.

(3) Realistically achievable.

(4) True indicators of outcome or output.

(5) Reflective of actual needs.

c. **Typical standards are rates** (e.g., cost per pound), limits (e.g., not more than and not less than), and criteria (e.g., fit and other forms of external interface standards, power, weight, volume, life, accuracy).

d. **Identification of systemic performance standards is recommended**. The more critical the result is to objective accomplishment, the more appropriate it is to develop a performance standard to evaluate that result. The level of detail must correspond to that expectation. Performance standards need not be identified explicitly if the requirement is so clearly stated that a standard for performance has been unmistakably established in the PWS or specification.

e. **Always consider the cost**. Applying performance standards appropriately should actually reduce overall costs as performance deficiencies are identified and improvements to these processes are made. Nevertheless, performance standards must be very selective and at the appropriate level. Do not spend money for performance standards you do not really need.

Always ask the questions:

(1) Is this level of detail necessary?
(2) What performance can be measured by querying the contractor's data system? (3) What is the risk of not having this level of performance?

f. **"Best value" is a combination of competitive pricing and improved performance.** Offerors should be encouraged to propose improvements above the minimum requirements and to propose lower cost alternatives that meet the performance criteria.

g. **Standards should be published and well recognized.** OMB Circular A-119 requires preference for national, international, or industry-wide standards. Standards developed by any agency with industry input may be used if technically suitable voluntary consensus standards are not available. This may be done through public meetings, public comment, or a Solicitation for Information per FAR 15.405 for government organizations.

Progress/Performance Measurement

a. Results can be measured by both progress and performance. Both are critical to effective management.

(1) **Progress** measurement identifies what you did, not necessarily how well you did it. The most typical example is milestone completion. For managing progress, either maintain or achieve a specific and definable performance level and/or requirement.

(2) **Performance** measurement identifies achievement of outcome or output in terms of quality, quantity, timeliness, and cost productivity.

b. **Performance** is measured by comparing the performance level against the range identified in the performance standards.. The standards must require performance reflecting the purchasing agency's minimum needs, failing which the objective of the contract will not be met. Standards cannot be level-of-effort or procedures. This approach has an inherent advantage because it allows far greater contractor flexibility in how to satisfy these performance requirements.

c. A **Performance Goal** is a target level of performance expressed as a tangible, measurable objective, against which actual achievement can be compared. A performance goal may be expressed as an absolute or as a range of acceptable performance (usually expressed in percentages); for example:

d. Such a measurement process could include multiple data points over time, be as quantitatively measurable as possible, and provide early identification of potential problems with the process, product, or service allowing management intervention. It often facilitates continuous improvement.

If there are a number of tasks and deliverables, summarize them within a PRS. List the contract and work requirements considered to be most critical to satisfactory contract performance, such as tasks, deliverables, and quality levels. Provide the minimum performance standard for each.

PBC PERFORMANCE INCENTIVES

GOALS AND OBJECTIVES

> **A contractor who only meets the minimum performance standards merits only a minimum fee.**

a. Performance-based contracting must assure that the purchaser obtains the products, services, and cost savings that it wants by providing tangible incentives that motivate the contractor to achieve levels of performance that exceed the minimum and have benefit to the purchaser. Many contractor (suppliers) will not necessarily move into this higher risk performance-based business realm unless they can anticipate a reward. Incentives must make it worthwhile to the contractor to find ways to improve performance.

b. Incentives are tools to improve the probability of better performance when the tasks are complex, critical, or have a history of performance or cost-overrun problems. A contract may include technical performance incentives when performance beyond the minimum is desirable, potentially achievable, and withstands the test of cost-benefit analysis.

c. The earning of incentives shall be based on a meaningful rating of the contractor's performance; normally, an objective measurement is preferred, however, some circumstances would allow for a subjective assessment. Where meaningful objectively measurable outcome criteria exist, combine cost incentives (CPIF and FPIF) and performance incentive provisions in preference to cost-plus-award-fee (CPAF).

d. For service-type contracts, reduction schedules may be used where appropriate.

INCENTIVE CRITERIA

a. Incentive criteria must be focused on program/project objectives. Contractor (supplier) input shall be obtained through the draft RFP process.

b. The contractor's performance in meeting major program objectives will be measured utilizing explicit, predefined criteria, such as the following:

> (1) Incentives must be relevant to performance. Follow-up must be accomplished to ensure that desired results are achieved; i.e., establish measures to determine the extent to which performance is actually achieved.

> (2) The criteria for incentives must center on the areas of value to the purchasing agency and those of high risk that are within the control of the contractor or supplier. Do not provide the contractor an incentive for work that is the responsibility of purchasing personnel.

> (3) Reasonable and attainable targets must be established, which are clearly communicated to the contractor.

> (4) The purchasing agency must benefit significantly from performance above the minimum.

> (5) The cost of the incentives must be less than or equal to the added value of the enhanced performance.

(6) They must be consistent with contract requirements and other program documents.

(7) They must be measurable and the measurement systems must be reliable.

(8) The contractor should not earn a big incentive for a small, easily reached achievement.

THE BOTTOM LINE:

"When a performance incentive is used, it shall be structured to be both positive and negative based on hardware performance after delivery and acceptance. In doing so, the contract shall establish a standard level of performance based on the salient mission performance requirement. This standard performance level is normally the contract's minimum performance requirement. No incentive amount is earned at the standard performance level. Discrete units of measurement based on the same performance parameter shall be identified for performance both above and below the standard. Specific incentive amounts shall be associated with each performance level from maximum beneficial performance (maximum positive incentive) to minimal beneficial performance or total failure (maximum negative incentive). The relationship between any given incentive, both positive and negative, and its associated unit of measurement must reflect the value to the Government of that level of hardware performance. Suppliers are not to be rewarded for above-standard performance levels that are of no benefit to the purchasing agency."

THE END

If you or your agency want training in how to properly develop a Performance Work Statement, give Mr. Robert Knauer, CPCM CPPO, a call or email him. Information about Robert Knauer CPCM CPPO can be found at www.LINKEDIN.com